ISBN: 9798391352303

www.jacquihutchinson.co.uk

* * *

For Sweet B and all the children
who are understanding their journey from their
Tummy Mummy to their Forever Homes:

Know your heart is so very loved.
Know that your story is important.
Know your journey has a beginning:

That you were loved along the way
and that the rest of the story is yours to tell.

* * *

This is where your story starts;
Inside your Tummy Mummy.
You kicked, and
stretched,
and tickled, and slept.ᶻᶻᶻ

You were, oh, so very funny!

Inside your   Tummy Mummy

Grew your heart   that was so loved.

And a piece of her   heart GREW in yours,

and fitted   like a glove.

Out you popped, a bundle of joy,
Ready for love and cuddles.
But your **Tummy Mummy** needed help
From all **her life's big troubles.**

So a **social worker** came to help,
And brought you to our home.
The place was **new**
and you felt **scared,**
You felt a bit **alone.**

But you soon began to realise,

Things weren't actually so bad,

You started feeling

safe and happy

Instead of feeling sad.

You made us laugh and giggle
As you sang and danced and played,
As you **stomped** and **roared**
like dinosaurs
Despite the mess you **made.**

You love to eat spaghetti,

And you love to bake and cook,

You love to play guitar,

And build a den and read a book.

You love your **foster home**
And soon found all the treats...
You ate a pot of **jam**
And stuffed **dry cereal** in your cheeks.
You were **filling up a hole**
That you didn't know was there.
You missed your **tummy mummy**
And wondered why she wasn't there.

But oh, how loved you are sweet child,
you really needn't worry,
when you look inside your heart,
you'll find a part of **tummy mummy**.
And oh, **how loved you are** sweet child,
by your **foster family** too...

(even when you had a bath,
and chose to do a poo!)

And oh, how loved you are sweet child by...

your family and friends,
your friends from school,
and **teachers** too,
the list just never ends.

but here's the thing that's **really hard**,
You're not our child to keep.
You've been in someone else's dreams
Each night when they're asleep.

your forever mum and daddy
cannot wait to come and meet you,
a **child** their **heart's** been missing
who can make all **their dreams come true.**

Only now it's getting **tricky**

and your **feelings** are all *strange*.

you don't quite know **what's happening**

or what has been arranged.

It's ok to feel **sad** and **scared**

You want to stay, you're just **frustrated.**

And it's fine to be **excited**

After all this time you've waited...

For a place to call **forever**,

For a place you can call **home**

For a **forever mum and daddy**

Who can call your **heart** their own.

And oh, how loved you are sweet child,

And of course we'll miss you so

Just look inside your heart my dear,

If you miss us when you go...

A piece of us is there inside

With Tummy Mummy's part,

You live In us and we in you

We're in each other's hearts.

So let your rainbow heart shine bright,
Full of love for all to see,
In the place that you can now call home,
With your forever family.

A Guide To Reading This Book

This book is a beautiful tool to help looked After Children explore their own story. Oh, How Loved You Are lends itself to being read on its own, or alongside the child's life book that the Social Worker should have given them as they begin the process of moving from foster care into permanency of adoption. Key phrases used throughout the book:

'Tummy Mummy'

A phrase used by social workers for littles to call their birth mother. She is the key in allowing a child to discover their identity and where they came from. Without Tummy Mummy, this much wanted, much needed child would not be here. Her story of why she could not look after her child is important and is told in a way that is easy for the child to understand at this age. By recognising Tummy Mummy and the forever place she has in the child's heart, empowers the child's sense of self, self-worth, identity, and their deep set, intrinsic need to know they are loved.

'Social Worker'

Older children who are over 12 months should recognise and know their social worker and have some sort of a relationship with them. The social worker is important to their story as it is the social worker who has taken them out of a place of chaos/danger and into a place of calm and safety. Their role should be seen and talked about positively in order for them to accept their own personal story and the need for them to be kept safe.

'Foster Home & Family'

The child's safe place, the people who fight for them, nurture them, protect them and keep them safe while their forever family is found. What an important part of their life and their story foster carers are. The child in your care will know who you are and will trust you and your decisions for them. They will know and trust others outside your immediate household because of their own attatchment to you. It is important for the child, therefore, that you speak positively of all who are involved in their story. Little ears absorb what is said as you talk about tummy mummy, Social workers and their new Forever mummy and daddy. By speaking positively into this, they are acknowledging that this is a place where they will feel loved and secure because of what you have said. Your role in developing the new relationships is of absolute paramount importance and so valuable.

The child will grieve the foster carers as they come to accept that they aren't their forever family. Foster Carers should still play a part in the child's life as advised by Adoption for Central England guidelines, which will help the child to know they weren't abandoned, or rejected. This grief that the child will go through may also trigger emotions from past trauma when they were separated from birth family, or various other trauma that they endured in their home. This grieving process is important as this leads them into a place of acceptance and may show itself at any time throughout their life.
Challenging as it may be, when they are grieving during the transition, the role of the foster carer to emotionally support the child throughout the transition period is paramount. The foster carer will help to navigate the emotions and comfort the child as and when needed and will give them the tools the child will need to manage their emotions once they have moved on.

It is also appropriate and encouraged for the adopters to talk about the foster carers positively and encouragingly with the child, that you're thankful they took care of the child whilst they found them. This will help to bridge the gap of the child feeling lost and worried about where they have gone. The foster family will also grieve. Foster carers go through secondary trauma during this process as they experience the feelings and distress of the child first hand and they come to terms with the fact that the child is moving on, that their 'job' has come to an end and as they start to live a new 'normal'. There will be a whole host of emotions; sadness, anger, relief, happiness, worry; Allow yourself the time to ride these emotions and to grieve the child you have just invested your heart into for a substantial period of time.

'Forever Family'

A heart that they are able to call their own. The child's new forever family have been hoping and counting down the days when this child can come 'home'. It is really important to highlight to the child that they are chosen. That out of all the children that could be adopted, their forever mummy and daddy have chosen them and they are someone that their forever family wants and needs. The child will absorb this, helping to soften the trauma of separation knowing that they are going into a family where they are wanted, longed for and needed. Their forever family are to be celebrated and spoken of often. Putting up pictures of their new family around the house will help to encourage conversation and get the child to become more familiar as well as showing them that the foster family accepts and welcomes them by putting up pictures in their own home. A lot is said about the trauma of an adopted child, but let it also be said, that the love of the adoptive family can, and will, go a long way towards the healing process of both the heart and mind! Love is a powerful tool for healing, joy and flourishing!!

'Thoughts and feeling'

Throughout the book, there are many thoughts and feelings that are named that the child can relate to, recognise and respond to. By naming the thoughts and feelings going on, it empowers the child to recognise their own feelings and allows them to be seen and heard. It opens up an opportunity for you to talk about how they are feeling and how you can help them to navigate and process their feelings. The thoughts and feelings of the child in your care, whether as a foster carer or an adopter, will most likely change each time you read the book, and that is absolutely fine, transition is a process and so are their feelings. Encourage an open conversation and support the child as they talk to you and name their feelings.

The importance of 'The heart balloon'

Throughout the book, the child carries around a heart balloon. This never leaves the child and is with them from the moment they are born, always growing and getting not only bigger but also more colourful. This heart is a symbol and a metaphor of how they carry a piece of everyone's heart and how those who have loved them not only hold a special place in their heart, but have given them a piece of their own heart. The balloon journeys with the child through their life and will continue go with them and grow beyond the transition to permanency. This is a great chance for you to talk to them about people in their life; who else do they love? Who else loves them? Who is going to love them? Who still loves them? Who can they add into their own heart that isn't named in the book to take with them forever?

This can also open up into an activity where they can make a heart, decorate it and fill it with the names or pictures of those they love and those who love them. This could go into their life book. They could also make and decorate their own hearts to give out to special people they met along their journey who they might be saying goodbye to.

The imagery of the heart is a profound visual reminder that the child is wanted and lovable; that they were not just loved, but 'oh SO loved' by so many. This is fundamental in their processing and acceptance of their story, which, ultimately, can help to minimise the separation trauma and feeling of rejection that they may go through during the adoption process or later on in life. Every child deserves the right to be loved. To know that their story is important. And above all, to know that, despite their situation, they themselves are good. They themselves, are wanted. And that they themselves, are loved.

Printed in Great Britain
by Amazon